The Library of
Political Assassinations

The Assassination of
Malcolm X

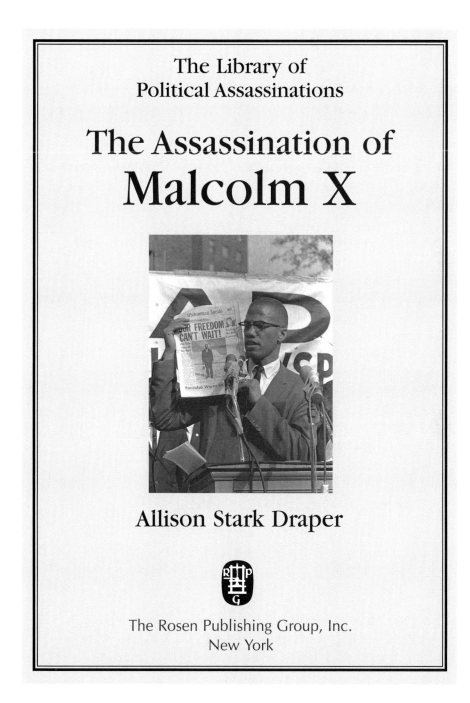

Allison Stark Draper

The Rosen Publishing Group, Inc.
New York

Published in 2002 by The Rosen Publishing Group, Inc.
29 East 21st Street, New York, NY 10010

Library of Congress Cataloging-in-Publication Data

Draper, Allison Stark.
The assassination of Malcolm X / by Allison Stark Draper. — 1st ed.
p. cm. — (The library of political assassinations)
Includes bibliographical references and index.
ISBN 0-8239-3542-6
1. X, Malcolm, 1925–1965—Assassination. 2. African American
Muslims—Biography.
I. Title. II. Series.
BP223.Z8 L573337 2002
364.15'24'092—dc21

2001003323

Manufactured in the United States of America

(Previous page) Malcolm X, leader of the black separatist
organization the Nation of Islam, at a rally in Harlem, New
York, in 1963. He played a major role in the civil rights
movement of the 1960s and 1970s.

Contents

Introduction 5

Chapter 1 The Assassination 9

Chapter 2 The Making of Malcolm X 14

Chapter 3 Minister Malcolm X 24

Chapter 4 The Death of Malcolm X 38

Chapter 5 The Assassination Revisited 47

Glossary 54
For More Information 57
For Further Reading 60
Index 62

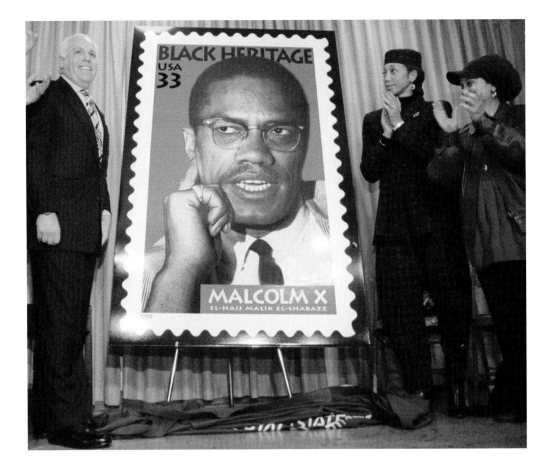

Malcolm X's daughter Attallah Shabazz *(second from right)* looks on during the rededication ceremony of the commemorative Malcolm X postage stamp in Philadelphia on February 5, 1999.

Introduction

In the early 1950s, the United States was racially segregated. African Americans and whites drank from different water fountains. They used different bathrooms and attended different schools. Usually, the facilities for whites were far superior to those for African Americans. Many African Americans objected to this injustice. They wanted Congress to pass a civil rights bill that would protect the rights of every American citizen, regardless of race. Their objections led to the creation of the civil rights movement, in which Americans protested against discrimination using such nonviolent methods as rallies and sit-ins. The majority of these protestors believed that integration—the equal participation of blacks and whites in American society—was essential to the creation of a truly free and democratic America.

Not everyone agreed. Some African Americans were convinced that integration would not lead to equality. They believed that integrating blacks into white society would not change the fact that America was a country defined and controlled by whites. These people wanted to create their own black society. They believed in separatism. Separatists choose to remove themselves from the mainstream. Some African American separatists argued that a separate black state with its own independent government and economy would provide African Americans with true liberation.

One black separatist organization that rose to power during the years of the civil rights movement was the Nation of Islam (NOI). Also known as Black Muslims, members of the NOI practiced a version of Islam, a major world religion in North Africa and the Middle East. The NOI adopted beliefs regarding worship, behavior, and dietary habits that reflected the convictions of traditional Islam.

Like traditional Muslims, Nation of Islam members believed in one god, Allah. They did not drink alcohol, use drugs, swear, dance, commit adultery, or eat pork. Men dressed conservatively, and women covered their hair. Unlike traditional Muslims, however, Black Muslims held certain convictions particular to the NOI.

NOI leaders taught followers that all of the peoples of the world were originally black. Whites were the result of a breeding experiment. Embittered against Allah, a brilliant but evil scientist had progressively lightened the skin of a community by forcing the palest people to marry and procreate. Each generation of children was paler than the last. As these people grew more pale, they grew less moral. Eventually, these white "devils" took over the world. They oppressed all nonwhite peoples—among them Africans, Asians, Arabs, and Indians—by taking their lands or forcing them into slavery.

The NOI believed that integration was not only undesirable but wrong. They argued that no one, black or white, really wanted integration. It led to hate and confusion. Their plan was for the 22 million African Americans in the United States to secede. They wanted to take over two or three states and create their own economic and social infrastructure that would include a government, businesses, schools, and temples.

The ideas of the NOI were extreme, but the unity the NOI offered to African Americans was appealing. The NOI taught black people to be proud of their blackness. They offered shelter from the hurricane of racism and white supremacy in the United States, and countered the popular white notion that black people were biologically inferior to whites.

Within the NOI, African Americans found respect and support. They also found a strict behavioral code. The NOI recognized and fought the damage inflicted by alcohol and drug addiction in inner-city neighborhoods. They helped people overcome their addictions and reconstruct their lives. They also reached out to convicts, many of whom they believed had been mistreated by the white-controlled justice system.

The NOI message that America was viciously racist and that black dignity was possible spoke to many African Americans in prison. One of these was a man named Malcolm Little. Little joined the NOI and replaced what he considered his slave surname with an *X*. From then on, he was known as Malcolm X.

Malcolm X became a minister of the Nation of Islam. He preached the word of the Black Muslims and raised their membership into the thousands. His condemnation of racism and praise of black people helped create a new vocabulary of pride and identity for many African Americans.

Malcolm X was an orator. He spent thirteen years infuriating and inspiring his listeners as he spoke against injustice. His was a life of words, and his words were profoundly important. They opened the door to revelation, revolution, and constructive change.

In his early years as a Black Muslim, Malcolm X firmly believed that radical separatism was the route to freedom and opportunity for African Americans. He was convinced that true black liberation lay in self-sufficiency. Later in his life, he began to see the potential for racial cooperation. This shift in belief followed his break with the NOI and, before his death, raised the possibility that he might cooperate with such mainstream civil rights activists as Dr. Martin Luther King Jr.

In pursuit of political and spiritual truth, Malcolm X traveled to Mecca, the Muslim holy site in Saudi Arabia. Afterward, he changed his name to El-Hajj Malik El-Shabazz. This is the name that his wife, Betty, had engraved on his tombstone when he died. Had he lived, perhaps El-Shabazz would have built a cultural bridge between African Americans and Muslims in Africa and the Middle East. Or, he might have worked for political change with Dr. King. Instead, on February 21, 1965, at the age of thirty-nine, Malcolm X was assassinated.

The Assassination

On Sunday February 21, 1965, at 2:00 PM, Malcolm X was scheduled to speak at the Audubon Ballroom at the intersection of 166th Street and Broadway in Harlem, New York. He had spent the previous night at the Hilton hotel in Manhattan. At eight o'clock on Sunday morning, the phone rang in Malcolm's room. He picked up the receiver and heard a man say, "Wake up, brother!" Then the phone went dead. The call unnerved him. Malcolm knew that he had enemies. He phoned his wife, Betty, and told her about the strange call. He also asked that she and their four children come to the ballroom to hear him speak.

At one o'clock, Malcolm left the hotel. He drove to Harlem, parked his car twenty blocks from the Audubon, and waited for a bus to take him the rest of the way. While he waited, a car pulled up and a man inside waved to him. One of the men in the car was Charles Blackwell, a Muslim in Malcolm's organization, Muslim Mosque, Inc. Malcolm got into the car. As they headed to the Audubon, Malcolm's security guards took their positions in and around the ballroom. At that point, people were already seated near the stage. Among them was a man named Talmadge Hayer (also known as Thomas Hagan) and, allegedly, two men named Thomas 15X Johnson and Norman 3X Butler. Johnson and Butler were both active members of the Nation of Islam.

For several months, Malcolm had prevented his guards from searching members of his audiences. He felt that searching people created an atmosphere of fear and hate. Outside, twenty police officers stood guard. Most of them, in accordance with Malcolm's orders, were in the hospital across the street rather than in full view of the entrance.

Arriving at the Audubon

Malcolm and a few supporters arrived at the Audubon at 2:00 PM. Backstage, Malcolm expressed doubt about the meeting. He was tired and curt, which was unlike him. He felt exhausted and discouraged. His aides watched him with concern. As they waited, the guest speakers Malcolm had invited to speak at the event began to cancel. One after another, they phoned with excuses.

Malcolm sat gloomily in the anteroom and then leapt up. Too tense to sit, he started pacing. Several people tried to comfort him and were startled by his sharp responses to their concern. Malcolm waited backstage; his aide, Benjamin Goodman, began an opening speech in which he introduced Malcolm to the audience. Malcolm remarked that he had a feeling he should not go onstage.

When Goodman finished, Malcolm walked onto the stage. He offered the Muslim greeting: "As salaam alaikum" ("Peace be unto you"). The audience replied: "Wa alaikum as salaam" ("And unto you be peace"). Immediately following the greetings, a disturbance erupted. One man snarled at another, "Get your hand out of my pocket!"

Malcolm urged the men to remain calm. His guards moved toward the scuffle. Malcolm stood alone at the podium. Toward the back of the room, a smoke bomb—a homemade device of crumbled safety matches and film wrapped in two handkerchiefs and stuffed inside a sock soaked in lighter fluid—exploded and began filling the room with smoke.

Abruptly, a man standing in point-blank range of the stage pulled a sawed-off shotgun from under his coat and shot Malcolm in the chest. He was so close that the shotgun pellets hit Malcolm's body within a seven-inch circle. Blood stained the middle of Malcolm's white shirt. Malcolm grabbed his chest and fell backward, cracking his head on the stage. The gunman fired again. Two other men, armed with pistols, rushed forward and shot repeatedly into Malcolm's stilled body.

The Aftermath

The murderers ran from the room firing their guns. People ducked and screamed. Betty (who was pregnant with twins) hid her four children under a bench and

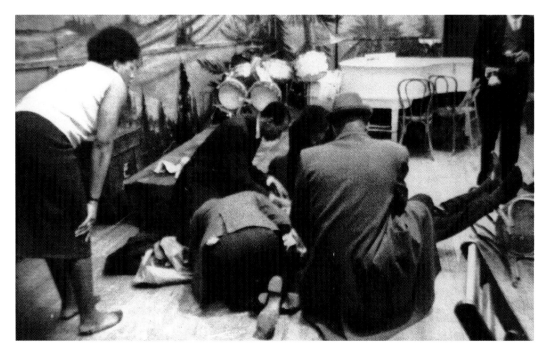

Malcolm X's followers tend to him as he lies mortally wounded on the stage of the Audubon Ballroom in Harlem.

covered them with her body. One of the assassins escaped through a rest room. The other two sprinted toward the stairs. One was almost stopped by a man whose punch knocked him down the staircase. Gene Roberts, an undercover cop posing as one of Malcolm's protégés, hit the other fleeing assassin with a chair. This was Talmadge Hayer. When Hayer got up, Reuben Francis (Malcolm's head of security) shot him in the leg. Hayer struggled to reach the stairs and slid along the banister until the crowd seized him and started pummeling him. They would have killed him, but two police officers coming to investigate the disturbance seized and arrested him.

Several people tried to revive Malcolm. Gene Roberts tried to give him cardiopulmonary resuscitation (CPR), as did a nurse who was also on the stage. Betty, a registered nurse, rushed up to help, saw that it was too late, and fell to her knees beside her husband's body. According to reports, she removed a piece of paper from his pocket that listed five men he believed might try to assassinate him.

Someone brought a stretcher from the hospital across the street. Malcolm was loaded onto it and rushed to the emergency room. It was 3:15 PM. By 3:30, having cut open Malcolm's chest and massaged his heart, the attending surgeons gave up. A member of the hospital staff emerged to speak to Betty and the people gathered around. He said, "The gentleman you know as Malcolm X is dead. He died from gunshot wounds. He was apparently dead before he got here. He was shot in the chest several times and once in the cheek."

Police and supporters carry Malcolm X on a stretcher after he was shot in the Audubon Ballroom.

2

The Making of Malcolm X

Malcolm X often said that he would die a violent death. His family had a history of bloody deaths. Four of his six uncles had died violently, three at the hands of white men (one by lynching). His father was probably murdered by white supremacists.

Born on May 19, 1925, in Omaha, Nebraska, Malcolm X was christened Malcolm Little. His father, the Reverend Earl Little, was a Baptist minister. Reverend Little was an African American activist. He worked for the Universal Negro Improvement Association (UNIA). A Jamaican leader named Marcus Garvey founded the UNIA. Garvey argued that there was no future for African Americans in the United States. Garvey organized a "back to Africa" movement advocating the return of African Americans to their ancestral homeland.

Not long after Malcolm's birth, the Littles moved from Omaha to Lansing, Michigan. A few years after that, Malcolm lost his father. According to *The Autobiography of Malcolm X*, one afternoon in 1931 Malcolm witnessed a fight between his parents.

His mother, Louise, was cooking dinner. His father ended the argument by storming out of the house and heading up the road. Just as he walked out, Louise had a vision of her husband's death. She trusted her ability to sense things and ran out the door after him, calling his name. He turned and waved but kept going. For the rest of the day, Louise was rattled. She cried and hugged her children with an uncharacteristic intensity. By their bedtime, Earl had not returned.

That night, Malcolm was awakened by his mother's screams from the living room. The police had arrived. Reverend Little was dead. He had been found on the streetcar tracks. His

Marcus Garvey, founder of the Universal Negro Improvement Association, is shown opening the UNIA's annual world convention in New York on August 1, 1922.

skull was bashed in on one side and his body was cut nearly in half where the streetcar had run over him. (Later, one of the Littles' insurance companies, most likely in an effort to avoid paying benefits to Louise Little and her family, claimed that Reverend Little had committed suicide. Most people found it hard to believe a man could crush his own skull before lying down on the tracks to be hit by a streetcar.)

Sadly, the death of Earl Little meant the death of his family. Louise struggled to feed and care for her six children, but it was too much for one person. Eventually, against her will, social service officials took the children and placed them in foster homes.

School

Malcolm went to live with a white family. He did very well in school. He remained at the top of his class and became class president. When he was in the eighth grade, a teacher asked him what he would like to be when he grew up. Malcolm had not thought much about his future. He knew he did not enjoy washing dishes, which was what he did after school for pocket money. He told his teacher that he might become a lawyer. The teacher, looking surprised, advised against it. Malcolm should be realistic, he said; the law was not a likely profession for a black man. Malcolm was good with his hands; why not be a carpenter?

After this conversation, Malcolm learned from his white classmates that this teacher had supported all of their choices. His teacher had encouraged the hopes and dreams of white students with grades far below Malcolm's. Malcolm realized that his teacher saw his color before he saw his ability or his intelligence. At the end of the eighth grade, Malcolm dropped out of school. He moved to Boston to live with his half sister, Ella.

Unlike Lansing, Boston was a big city with a large African American community. In Ella's respectable neighborhood, Malcolm met African Americans who were educated and self-sufficient. At first, these conservative people seemed incredibly sophisticated to Malcolm. Soon, however, fourteen-year-old Malcolm (whose height and build made him look much older) was drawn to hipper areas of Boston. He hung out in bars and nightclubs, worked as a shoeshine boy in a dance palace, conked (straightened) his hair, and dressed in zoot suits. The slick men whose sharp clothes and ready money marked them as hustlers became his heroes.

The young Malcolm X wore zoot suits like the ones these young men are wearing in this 1943 photo.

A job as a cook on a train took Malcolm back and forth between Boston and New York City. New York seduced him completely. He moved to Harlem, found a room, and worked as a bartender. Known as Detroit Red (because of his Michigan origins and reddish hair and skin tone), Malcolm soon slipped across the line between legal employment and hustling. After he lost his bartending job, he ran numbers for the lottery. This meant that he took the numbers people wanted to bet on and paid them when they won. He also worked as a drug dealer and a pimp. Eventually, a dispute with another hustler known as West Indian Archie forced Malcolm to leave town. Fearing for his safety, he moved back to Boston.

In Boston, Malcolm's goal was to find a criminal profession that would provide high profits, low risk, and independence. He picked robbery. He put together a crew that included an old friend, a friend of his friend, Malcolm's white girlfriend, and her sister. The gang stole jewelry, silverware, fur coats, and Oriental rugs. They did well, grew careless, and eventually got caught. The sentence Malcolm received, for a first-time offense, was unusually harsh. Malcolm believed his severe sentence was due to the fact that the judge disapproved even more strongly of black men stealing with white women than he did of the actual thefts. The average sentence for Malcolm's crime was about two years. Malcolm was sentenced to eight to ten. He served six and a half.

These are Malcolm X's mug shots from his arrest in Boston in 1946. At the time, he was known as Malcolm Little and was only eighteen years old.

Prison

In prison, Malcolm resumed his education. He completed a correspondence course in English and then one in Latin. As his writing improved, he wrote more often to his siblings back in Michigan. One of them, Philbert, told him about an organization he had joined called the Nation of Islam. Philbert wrote that Islam was "the natural religion of the black man." Initially, Malcolm was underwhelmed by the concept. He responded sarcastically and then forgot all about the NOI.

The Life of Malcolm X

1925
Malcolm X is born as Malcolm Little in Omaha, Nebraska.

1931
Malcolm X's father, the Reverend Earl Little, is killed in Lansing, Michigan, presumably by local white supremacists.

1946
Malcolm X is sentenced to prison for armed robbery. He serves six and one-half years at the Charlestown State Prison, the Concord prison, and the Norfolk Prison Colony, an experimental rehabilitation jail with a library, all in Massachusetts.

1948–1949
Malcolm X joins the Nation of Islam while in prison.

1952
Malcolm X is released from prison and moves to Detroit.

1954
The *Brown v. Board of Education* Supreme Court decision mandates the desegregation of public schools.

Malcolm X is promoted to minister of the Nation of Islam's New York Temple Number Seven.

1955
Rosa Parks, a member of the NAACP, refuses to give up her seat in the whites-only section of a public bus in Montgomery, Alabama. This sets off a highly successful boycott of the city's bus system.

1958
Malcolm X marries Sister Betty X in Lansing. They have six daughters: Attallah (born in 1958), Qubilah (1960), Ilyasah (1962), Gamilah (1964), and twins Malaak and Malikah (1965).

1963
President John F. Kennedy is assassinated, and the Nation of Islam silences Malcolm X, allegedly for his remarks following Kennedy's death.

March 1964
Malcolm X leaves the Nation of Islam and starts Muslim Mosque, Inc.

April 1964
Malcolm X makes the hajj (pilgrimage) to Mecca and changes his name to El-Hajj Malik El-Shabazz.

June 1964
Malcolm X founds the Organization of Afro-American Unity (OAAU), a secular political group.

December 1964
Muhammad Speaks publishes a piece, allegedly authored by Louis Farrakhan, that reads as a death warrant for Malcolm X.

1965
In February, Malcolm X's house is firebombed.

1965
On February 21, Malcolm X prepares to speak at the Audubon Ballroom in Harlem and is assassinated by at least three men.

1966
In the case against the suspected assassins of Malcolm X, the jury returns a verdict of guilty of murder in the first degree for Talmadge Hayer, Norman 3X Butler, and Thomas 15X Johnson.

Not long after this exchange, Malcolm received a letter from his brother Reginald. Reginald did not mention religion but advised Malcolm that if he wanted to get out of prison, he should quit smoking and stop eating pork. Malcolm was intrigued. Malcolm assumed that Reginald had some hustle in mind that would trick the authorities into letting him go. He smoked the rest of an open pack of cigarettes and then quit smoking. Several days later, when pork was served at lunch, he passed. The inmate beside him was surprised. Malcolm said, "I don't eat pork."

Reginald visited Malcolm in person to tell him about the Nation of Islam and its leader, Elijah Muhammad. Malcolm listened. Reginald explained how white society had nearly erased African Americans from the history books. Malcolm remembered that his seventh-grade American history book had only one paragraph about African Americans.

Conversion

Soon, Malcolm was convinced that Elijah Muhammad was right. He entered the prison library and began to read. He read everything he could find about the history of Africans in America and Africa. He read Will Durant's *Story of Civilization*, H. G. Wells's *Outline of History*, W. E. B. DuBois's *The Souls of Black Folk*, Carter G. Woodson's *Negro*

History, and J.A. Rogers's *Sex and Race*. In all of these accounts, he learned how white people had oppressed the other races of the world. He also came to believe that many of his personal troubles stemmed from the effects of racism.

Prior to his introduction to the Nation of Islam, Malcolm believed that he had only two choices as an African American man: He could live as a parasite (a criminal) or as an Uncle Tom (a servant). The NOI taught Malcolm that he had another choice.

Dr. William Edward Burghardt Du Bois was an anthropologist and cofounder of the National Association for the Advancement of Colored People (NAACP).

Malcolm wrote to Elijah Muhammad and asked to join the NOI. In prison, he began trying to convert his fellow inmates. When he was released in 1952, he moved to Detroit, ready to take up his new life and new mission as a Black Muslim.

Minister Malcolm X

In Detroit, Malcolm attended the Nation of Islam's Detroit Temple Number One with his brother Wilfred and Wilfred's family. On the Sunday before Labor Day in 1952, he drove to Chicago Temple Number Two to hear Elijah Muhammad speak in person. Malcolm's connection with Elijah Muhammad was immediate. In Chicago, Malcolm received the *X* that replaced his surname, Little—a name given to his ancestors when they were slaves. He also received Muhammad's blessing to convert others.

Malcolm was astounded that there were empty seats in the small temple in Detroit. He set out immediately into the surrounding neighborhoods to show people the way of the Nation of Islam. In bars, in pool halls, and on the street, he preached the message of the NOI. He explained that there was an alternative to poverty, drugs, alcohol, and crime; there was a religion that embraced people who were proud to be black. Within a few months, Malcolm had tripled the membership of Detroit Temple Number One. In the summer of 1953, Elijah Muhammad made Malcolm the assistant minister of the temple.

Malcolm X was a dynamic public speaker and an inspiration to many African Americans fighting segregation.

Minister X

Malcolm rose swiftly through the ranks. He traveled constantly, preaching in Philadelphia, Springfield, and Hartford, opening another temple in Atlanta, and flying back and forth to Chicago to report to Muhammad. He became a full minister, founded temples in Boston and Philadelphia, and in June 1954 became the minister of New York Temple Number Seven in Harlem. New converts swelled his congregation from one weekly meeting to the next. New convert Betty Sanders joined the temple in 1956. She and Malcolm were married in 1958.

In the spring of 1959, an African American journalist named Louis Lomax contacted Malcolm to request an interview. Many whites also became interested in the growing phenomenon of the Nation of Islam. *The Mike Wallace Show*, a television talk show, wanted to record a piece on the NOI. With Muhammad's blessing, Malcolm agreed. The show was filmed in New York, Chicago, and Washington. It included clips of Muhammad and his ministers preaching their convictions about blacks and whites. This was an exciting development. National publicity would surely reach thousands of potential converts all over the country. Black Muslims also hoped that white people would see the sense and intelligence of Muhammad's teachings.

When the show aired in the late fall of 1959, it was a disappointment and a shock. Titled "The Hate That Hate Produced," it bombarded viewers with close-ups of stern black men preaching about white devils. These images were intercut with threatening shots of the Fruit of Islam—a group of NOI men used as a security team for the Nation of Islam. These shots depicted Muslim men with quasi-military training practicing judo and karate. The show also aired seemingly exotic footage (to an uninformed audience) of Muslim women in white scarves and gowns. This tipped off a wave of negative newspaper and magazine articles that portrayed the NOI as a militant cult that preached hatred of—and advocated violence against—white society.

In His Own Words

They called me "a teacher, a fomenter of violence." I would say point blank, "That is a lie. I'm not for wanton violence, I'm for justice. I feel that if white people were attacked by Negroes—if the forces of law prove unable, or inadequate, or reluctant to protect those whites from those Negroes—then those white people should protect and defend themselves from those Negroes, using arms if necessary. And I feel that when the law fails to protect Negroes from whites' attacks then those Negroes should use arms, if necessary, to defend themselves" . . . I am speaking against and my fight is against white racists. I firmly believe that Negroes have the right to fight against these racists, by any means that are necessary.

—From *The Autobiography of Malcolm X*

Malcolm X understood the power of the press and used this savvy to publicize and promote Islam.

Malcolm—surprised and resigned to a negative portrayal of a black liberation movement—still believed that all publicity was good publicity. Moreover, he had begun publishing his views. He wrote a small column first for the *Amsterdam News*, a local Harlem newspaper, and then for the *Los Angeles Herald Dispatch*. Eventually, he planned to start a Muslim paper for the NOI. After observing the production process at the *Herald Dispatch*, he set up a press in Harlem. He named his new NOI paper *Muhammad Speaks*. NOI members sold copies on street corners in African American neighborhoods all over the country.

During this time, the NOI also attracted positive interest. A Nigerian anthropologist named E. U. Essien-Udom, a professor at the University of Ibadon in Nigeria, wrote a book on the NOI, as did an African American professor of religion named Dr. C. Eric Lincoln, called *The Black Muslims in America*. While teaching in Atlanta, Lincoln had received a paper from a student who maintained that

Christianity was an impossible religion for African Americans to practice. The student argued that Christianity was a white religion whereas Islam was a black religion. Intrigued, Lincoln decided to research the NOI for a book. When Lincoln and Malcolm X met, Lincoln decided to arrange a speaking engagement for Malcolm X at Boston University. Soon, Malcolm was speaking at colleges and universities across the country.

Malcolm was a riveting speaker. He had a preacher's ability to speak for long periods with passion and emphasis. He was well-read and possessed a powerful memory. In addition, while in prison he had honed his debating skills in an educational rehabilitation program. There, he had often sparred with volunteers from Harvard University and Boston University.

Malcolm X's phone rang off the hook with requests from newspaper and magazine journalists. He spoke on radio shows and appeared on television panels. When Alex Haley interviewed him for *Playboy* magazine, the piece was printed in full. Malcolm could not believe that the white establishment had finally published his words, uncut. The Nation of Islam was truly being heard!

Tensions Within the NOI

Those close to Elijah Muhammad complained that Malcolm X was promoting himself at Muhammad's expense. For many years, Muhammad told them this was nonsense. He loved Malcolm X like a son. And Malcolm

Boxing champion Muhammad Ali (known at the time as Cassius Clay) watches Black Muslim leader Elijah Muhammad speak at a rally in New York City on June 28, 1964.

never spoke without giving credit to Muhammad. He once claimed that he always said Muhammad's name at least once a minute while speaking. Even so, the mainstream world of popular television news shows and *New York Times* articles portrayed Malcolm X as the voice and the leader of the Nation of Islam.

Further straining the once close relationship between Elijah Muhammad and Malcolm X was the fact that Malcolm's goals for the Nation of Islam did not precisely mirror Muhammad's. Malcolm wanted to start a voting drive. He believed that the 22 million African Americans in the United States should use their votes as a collective voice. This would make them a powerful political force in elections.

To organize the voting drive, Malcolm decided to cooperate with civil rights organizations such as the National Association for the Advancement of Colored People (NAACP), the Southern Christian Leadership Conference (SCLC), and the Congress of Racial Equality (CORE). In this way, Malcolm hoped to create a united black front. Without waiting for Muhammad's permission, Malcolm organized the drive.

Malcolm also believed in a level of militancy that Muhammad, at least publicly, did not advocate. Many Muslims insisted that their religion valued peace. Malcolm felt that self-defense was a reasonable response to the violent persecution many African Americans experienced in the United States. Citing the Communist revolutions in China (1949) and Russia (1917), Malcolm argued that political revolutions often involve a certain amount of bloodshed.

In 1963, President John F. Kennedy was assassinated. The event plunged most of the country into deep grief. Several hours after the shooting, Malcolm X spoke at the Harlem temple. While Kennedy was alive, Malcolm had considered him a self-serving white man, governing a nation that was run for and by white people. After the assassination, Malcolm described Kennedy—who did much to foster the civil rights movement, but not as much as he promised—as a segregationist and a "crook." Given the violent manner of Kennedy's death, Malcolm's comments shocked and offended many Americans.

Nine days later, Malcolm spoke to a crowd of 700. In the crowd, there were two white reporters. Malcolm let them stay. This went against Muhammad's recent decision to ban white people from Black Muslim gatherings. In his speech, Malcolm said that Kennedy had ignored the problems of African Americans. The assassination was a case of "chickens coming home to roost."

Even though Muhammad was probably not offended by Malcolm's statements regarding Kennedy, Muhammed wanted Malcolm brought under control. Malcolm's words gave Muhammad an excuse to silence him. The next day, Muhammad suspended Malcolm's rights as a minister of the Nation of Islam for ninety days.

El-Hajj Malik El-Shabazz

Suspended from the Nation of Islam, Malcolm struck out on his own. He set up a new mosque and named it Muslim Mosque, Inc. Then he held a press conference. He explained that his mosque would practice the true Islam of Africa and the Middle East. This spiritual base would support a political program. Through the mosque and work with other activists, he would combat the social and economic oppression of African Americans. After the press conference, Malcolm prepared himself for the hajj.

All Muslims are expected to try to make a pilgrimage, or hajj, to the holy city of Mecca in Saudi Arabia once in their lives. It is a religious duty. Those who are humanly able must make the trip.

In many ways, the hajj was a revelation for Malcolm. What astonished him most was the range of skin colors among the other pil-

While on the hajj in 1964, Malcolm had a revelation: He saw that a multiracial world existed outside of the United States in which people of color were treated as equals.

grims. Muslims were not only black or brown. Some were white, with blond hair and blue eyes. None of them, black or white, treated Malcolm like an inferior being. He felt as if he had walked outside for the first time in his life and breathed clean air. Outside of America, Malcolm discovered that a multiracial world existed in which black people were treated as equals.

During his travels, Malcolm met many pilgrims from all over the world. He also met a number of important political figures. In New York, Malcolm knew a man whose son, Omar Azzam, lived in Jedda, Saudi Arabia. Malcolm called Azzam for assistance with a passport issue. Immediately, he found himself welcomed into a world of wealthy, educated, and powerful Muslims. Azzam's sister was the wife of the son of Prince Faisal, the ruler of Saudi Arabia. All of these people treated Malcolm as a respected guest. Some were dark-skinned, others light-skinned. Among them, Malcolm felt the color barrier he had lived with all his life fade away.

This led Malcolm to conclude that discrimination against blacks in America was not the inevitable result of a mixed-race society. In America, racism was so deeply ingrained that it was almost the same as race. To be white was to be racist. To be black was to be oppressed.

Malcolm's travels revealed to him that societies could not only be integrated but also color-blind. Malcolm believed that the spiritual unity Islam inspired made color-blindness possible. For him, an integral part of true belief was the realization that skin color is unimportant.

After visiting Mecca, Malcolm traveled throughout the Middle East and Africa. He spoke at the University of Beirut in Lebanon. He flew to Egypt and then to Nigeria. In Lagos, Nigeria, he met Professor Essien-Udom, who had written about the Nation of Islam in his book *Black Nationalism*. Malcolm spoke at Ibadan University in Lagos and found that young African students—unlike many American students—thought globally about politics. These students were concerned about their black brothers and sisters in America.

Malcolm also appeared on African television shows and on the radio. African journalists informed Malcolm that United States officials often sent reports to the African media stating that conditions for African Americans were slowly but steadily improving. Malcolm told them that these reports were propaganda.

Finally, Malcolm flew to Ghana. He was welcomed into the country and invited to address the Ghanaian parliament. He met such African American expatriates as Julian Mayfield and Maya Angelou. Both Mayfield and Angelou were writers and critics who believed in the importance of recognizing a black cultural tradition. They discussed the idea of promoting a pan-African unity that would include African Americans as well as people from many countries in Africa. (At this time, many African countries had just won their independence from European imperial governments and were setting up their first postcolonial governments.)

When Malcolm X returned to America, he viewed the oppression of African Americans as a human rights problem. He considered all African Americans, not just Muslims, part of a black nation with ties to Africa. In the last months of his life, Malcolm decided to raise the issue of African American rights at the United Nations.

Through the United Nations, Malcolm hoped to make the world aware of how poorly the United States treated its black citizens. Friends warned him that it was madness to threaten the United States government and involve the international body in national affairs, but Malcolm never questioned his path. This was the end to which his activism and religion had led him.

Threats Increase

The Nation of Islam condemned Malcolm X. On December 1, 1964, *Muhammad Speaks* printed a piece stating that Malcolm was "worthy of death." As early as the fall of 1964, while he was still in Africa, Malcolm was convinced someone had tried to poison him. In February 1965, Malcolm received numerous threatening phone calls. On February 14, 1965, several Molotov cocktails were thrown through his living-room window as he and his family slept. Malcolm and Betty rushed the children outside and watched the house burn. Malcolm told the police that he thought the NOI may have been involved. There are many theories regarding who harassed and ultimately murdered Malcolm X. In addition to suspicions surrounding the Central Intelligence Agency (CIA) and the NOI, some people believe that the Mafia murdered Malcolm X because his antidrug crusade interfered with their profitable dope trade in Harlem.

Malcolm was invited to attend a conference in Bandung, Indonesia, and then return to Africa for an Organization of African Unity (OAU) summit in late February 1965. Had Malcolm lived to attend these meetings, he and his supporters would have compared the plight of blacks in America to that of blacks in South Africa, who suffered under the system of

Furniture damaged by a firebombing lies outside Malcolm X's home in Elmhurst, New York, on February 15, 1965.

segregation known as apartheid. Some journalists and historians believe that the CIA killed Malcolm to prevent his attendance. It would have been extremely embarrassing for the United States government to be publicly denounced as a racist regime comparable to that governing South Africa.

We may never know who was behind the killing of Malcolm X. What we do know is that he suspected that his speech at the Audubon Ballroom on February 21, 1965, would be his last. Despite this, he walked onto the stage that day and, ultimately, into a hail of gunfire.

Chapter 4

The Death of Malcolm X

The outpouring of grief in Harlem was immense. Between twenty and thirty thousand people said good-bye to Malcolm as he lay in a glass-lidded bronze casket at the Unity Funeral Home. The actor Ossie Davis gave a eulogy in which he described Malcolm as a man who fought racism and injustice as he breathed, a man who refused to compromise, and a man who would make you angry but who would also make you proud.

For some mourners, the pain of grief was indistinguishable from the desire for revenge. Late on the day following the assassination, the Nation of Islam's Fruit of Islam met at their Harlem mosque. After they left, three or four men climbed to the top of a neighboring building and crept onto the roof of the mosque. They broke a window, pitched in several Molotov cocktails, and ran. The building went up with a whoosh and a boom. The flames leapt thirty feet into the cold air. It took firefighters all night to put it out.

Among the NOI, there was no mourning at all. Saviour's Day, a national NOI holiday, fell five days after Malcolm X's death. In Chicago, Elijah

Malcolm X's body lies covered by a glass screen at the Unity Funeral Home in New York City on February 24, 1965. Tens of thousands of people paid their respects to the slain civil rights leader.

Muhammad preached that Malcolm had gotten what he deserved, nearly mirroring Malcolm's response to the assassination of President Kennedy.

Back in Harlem, the police struggled to find Malcolm's assassins. Talmadge Hayer was in custody; the police planned to arrest a suspect named Norman Butler. When they called NOI headquarters in Chicago to find out if Butler was a member of the Fruit of Islam, no one at the mosque seemed to know who he was. As far as the NOI were concerned, justice had been done. A police investigation did not interest them.

Whether Malcolm X had been killed because he was a religious threat to the NOI, a political threat to the United States government, or an obstacle to the organized drug trade did not affect the police investigators' overall view of Malcolm's death. They understood the assassination as a complicated homicide. They were not concerned with religious, racial, or international politics.

While many abroad, especially in Africa, mourned Malcolm's death, the United States government remained unsentimental. Many government officials had regarded Malcolm X as a troublemaker. Carl T. Rowan, head of the United States Information Agency at the time of the assassination, maintained that the grief expressed in Africa and around the world was the direct result of a failure to understand who Malcolm X was and what he represented. Those people, he said, in Ghana, Egypt, Saudi Arabia, and China did not realize that Malcolm X promoted hate and violence.

Nevertheless, the response from abroad was one of sincere and deep grief. The foreign leaders who had met Malcolm believed he was a visionary and a force for revolution. They hailed him as a martyr. Many believed the American government had silenced Malcolm.

People in Nigeria, Algeria, and Ghana, in China and Pakistan, in Indonesia and Cuba, mourned the death of Malcolm X. In most of these countries, his assassination was front-page news. In England, where Malcolm had made his last appearance abroad, students protested in front of the United States embassy. In London, too, editorials condemned the assassination. The American media neglected to reprint most of these pieces.

Our Shining Black Prince

Here at this final hour, in this quiet place Harlem has come to bid farewell to one of its brightest hopes extinguished now, and gone from us forever. For Harlem is where he worked and where he struggled and fought, his home of homes, where his heart was, and where his people are—and it is, therefore, most fitting that we meet once again in Harlem to share these last moments with him . . . However we may have differed with him—or with each other about him and his value as a man—let his going from us serve only to bring us together, now. Consigning these mortal remains to earth, the common mother of all, secure in the knowledge that what we place in the ground is no more now a man but a seed which, after the winter of our discontent, will come forth again to meet us. And we will know him then for what he was and is— a Prince—our own black shining Prince!—who didn't hesitate to die, because he loved us so.

—Eulogy delivered by Ossie Davis at the funeral of Malcolm X, at the Faith Temple Church of God, on February 27, 1965

The Investigation

As much of the world mourned, the police got on with the investigation. News of the shooting reached Manhattan North Homicide shortly after three o'clock on February 21. The police on the scene had one person in custody. They had captured suspected gunman Talmadge Hayer. A bullet had hit Hayer in the leg as he ran from the room, causing him to fall. Had the police not intervened, the enraged crowd would probably have killed him.

Detectives on the scene went to the hospital, found Malcolm dead in the emergency room, and headed across the street to the Audubon Ballroom. A few dozen spectators were still milling around the area. Inside the ballroom, police officers handled the remains of the smoke bomb, chalked marks around the bullet holes, and dug slugs out of the wood.

Ballistics experts identified the bullets. At least three guns had been fired: a 12-gauge shotgun, a .45, and a 9 mm automatic—probably a Luger. The police found the 12-gauge Sears Roebuck shotgun, with its double barrels sawed from thirty inches down to eight and a half. It was short enough to hide under a winter coat. The .45 and the Luger were still missing.

At the police station, officers interviewed witnesses for their versions of the assassination. Many of the African Americans who had been at the Audubon did not trust cops. This distrust stemmed in part from a history of racist mistreatment by the police and the entire criminal justice system. Some witnesses believed that law enforcement officials, either FBI or CIA agents, had masterminded the assassination. Still other people blamed the police for failing to protect Malcolm. Even the testimonies of the witnesses who did cooperate were hampered by the smoke, noise, and chaos that had engulfed the scene of the shooting. Many remained unsure of what they had seen.

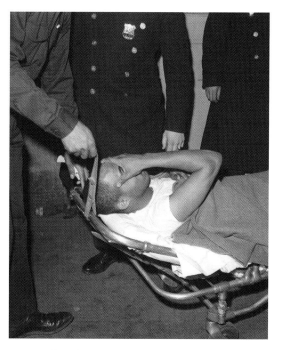

Stretcher-borne Talmadge Hayer (also known as Thomas Hagan) covers his face with his hand as police take him from Jewish Memorial Hospital.

As the investigation continued, detectives slowly pieced together a sequence of events. They knew that a man had drawn the audience's attention away from Malcolm X's speech by yelling. Then a smoke bomb had exploded. Malcolm's guards had moved away from him to investigate. As Malcolm stood unprotected, the killers approached the stage and fired. Then, in the confusion, they dashed toward the exits in a blaze of bullets.

Based on evidence that three guns had been used, the police decided there were three assassins. When they found Talmadge Hayer's thumbprint on a piece of the smoke bomb, they arrested him for murder. Now they needed two more suspects and a motive.

The police were fairly certain that the Nation of Islam was involved in the assassination. They believed this because of the break between Malcolm and the NOI and because Malcolm himself had predicted such an attempt. Elijah Muhammad, speaking from NOI headquarters in Chicago, claimed to have no knowledge of the event. He described the incident as a tragedy that Malcolm had brought upon himself. Muhammad's associates said they had never heard of Talmadge Hayer. Hayer himself insisted that he was not a Black Muslim.

Butler and Johnson

Relying on the varied testimony of witnesses, the police narrowed their search to two men: Norman 3X Butler and Thomas 15X Johnson. Butler and Johnson said they were innocent. Butler insisted that he could not have been involved because he had a medical condition that made it difficult for him to walk. Johnson claimed to have been at home all day on February 21.

There was no physical evidence to link either man to the scene. Police did not find their fingerprints on the weapons. They had no connection to Hayer. In

On the left, police escort Norman 3X Butler to jail in New York City. On the right, Thomas 15X Johnson *(center)* is charged in the slaying of Malcolm X.

addition, they were both known members of the NOI and openly hostile toward Malcolm X. Had they been at the Audubon, Malcolm's guards would almost certainly have taken note and watched their every move. Nevertheless, the police arrested Butler and Johnson.

The Trial

On January 12, 1966, Hayer, Butler, and Johnson went to trial charged with the murder of Malcolm X. At the trial, the lawyers for the defense insisted that the men had no motive. The prosecution countered, arguing that Hayer was indeed a Black Muslim and therefore linked with Butler and Johnson. Prosecutors also found eyewitnesses to place both Butler and Johnson at the scene. One of these witnesses claimed he saw Johnson stand up out of the audience with a shotgun in his hands. Another said he saw Butler fighting his way out of the crowd after the shooting rampage ended.

On February 28, 1966, Hayer confessed. He told the court he had been in the Audubon Ballroom and had fired four shots from a .45 into the body of Malcolm X. Hayer stated that a person, whom he would not name, had offered him a large sum of money to kill Malcolm X. Hayer insisted that this person was not affiliated with the Nation of Islam.

He also insisted that Johnson and Butler were not involved in the shooting. According to Hayer, four other men had taken part. Two sat in the front row with pistols, one sat in the fourth row with a shotgun, and one sat in the back. The man in the back started the commotion, yelling, "Get your hand out of my pocket!" Then the man in the fourth row stood up and shot Malcolm X with a shotgun. The two men in front fired their pistols. Hayer refused to identify these four men.

The jury was skeptical. They believed that Hayer, who knew he was facing life in jail anyway, was just trying to set Butler and Johnson free. After twenty hours and twenty minutes, the jury returned with their verdict. They found Hayer, Butler, and Johnson guilty of murder in the first degree.

The Assassination Revisited

During the years following the assassination of Malcolm X, the United States was torn by rioting, police brutality, and student protest. Groups that began as forces for positive change, like the Black Panthers, the Student Nonviolent Coordinating Committee (SNCC), and Students for a Democratic Society (SDS), rose to power and then fell prey to government sabotage and clashes with one another.

They also contended with increasing (and often illegal) FBI surveillance. The FBI blamed militant African American organizations such as the Black Panthers for outbreaks of racial violence. The FBI terrorized and infiltrated these groups, often working with local police. For years, the FBI had routinely tapped the phones and occasionally bugged the homes and meeting places of such African American leaders as Malcolm X and Dr. Martin Luther King Jr. In December 1969, a police raid in Chicago led to the deaths of two Black Panther leaders, Fred Hampton and Mark Clark. Partially as a result of this harassment, by the late 1970s many revolutionary groups had disbanded or disintegrated.

The appointment did not last. In late July 1999, Farrakhan was fighting prostate cancer. The National Board of Laborers, the group he set up to run the NOI in his absence, removed Aziz from his post.

Malcolm X Lives

For those who believed in him, the aftermath of Malcolm X's assassination was a desolate time. Something irreplaceable had been lost. His death weakened many people's belief in the possibility for change. Dr. Martin Luther King Jr., who had not always agreed with Malcolm X, saw it as a particular tragedy that Malcolm should have died just as he was moderating his formerly separatist views. Dr. King also praised Malcolm's courage, remarking, "One has to conquer the fear of death if he is going to do anything constructive in life and take a stand against evil."

This courage is Malcolm's legacy. Malcolm was a relentlessly provocative revolutionary. His conviction, intelligence, and intensity struck fear into the hearts of his opponents. Malcolm X spoke his mind, to both black and white America, without fear or compromise, inspiring many of the political activists and revolutionaries who followed. The Black Power movement came alive in a generation of African Americans who had heard Malcolm X speak.

To millions of Americans, Malcolm X remains an inspirational figure in the fight for equal rights.

Had Malcolm X lived, he might well have continued his journey as the pan-Africanist El-Shabazz. What his assassination stole from him—and from us—is this possibility. What it cannot take away is the Malcolm X we already have. His enduring words and image on posters and T-shirts remind us that battling injustice is a duty. We must recognize what jails us and act to free ourselves, by any means necessary. Malcolm survived crime, drug addiction, poverty, and prison. Then he rebuilt himself. He recognized his oppression, denounced it, and turned his conviction outward. His gift to us is his belief that the same struggles that can transform an individual can also transform the world.

An Era of Change

1947
Jackie Robinson joins the Brooklyn Dodgers, breaking the color barrier in major league baseball.

1948
Malcolm Little is introduced to Nation of Islam teachings while in prison.

1954
The Supreme Court issues its decision in *Brown v. Board of Education*, declaring segregated school facilities for black and white students illegal.

1955
Rosa Parks, a member of the NAACP, refuses to give up her seat in the whites-only section of a public bus in Montgomery, Alabama. This sets off a highly successful boycott of the city's bus system.

Malcolm X becomes minister of New York Temple Number Seven.

1957
Dr. Martin Luther King Jr. becomes president of the Southern Christian Leadership Conference (SCLC), organized to coordinate civil rights activities.

1959
The television documentary "The Hate That Hate Produced" airs nationally on *The Mike Wallace Show*.

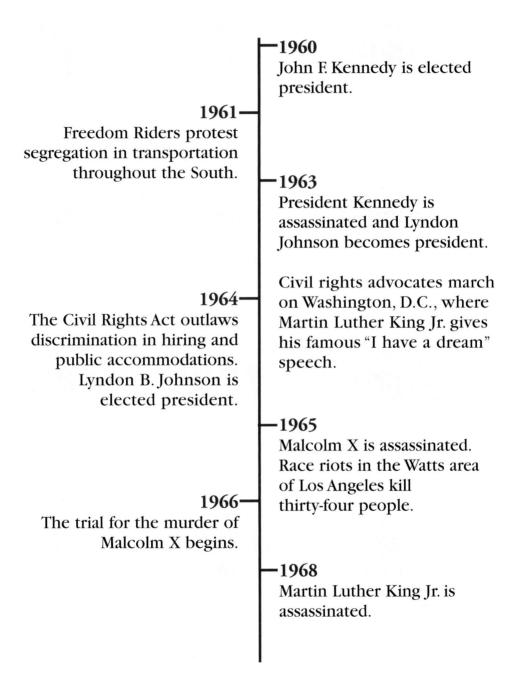

1960
John F. Kennedy is elected president.

1961
Freedom Riders protest segregation in transportation throughout the South.

1963
President Kennedy is assassinated and Lyndon Johnson becomes president.

Civil rights advocates march on Washington, D.C., where Martin Luther King Jr. gives his famous "I have a dream" speech.

1964
The Civil Rights Act outlaws discrimination in hiring and public accommodations. Lyndon B. Johnson is elected president.

1965
Malcolm X is assassinated. Race riots in the Watts area of Los Angeles kill thirty-four people.

1966
The trial for the murder of Malcolm X begins.

1968
Martin Luther King Jr. is assassinated.

Glossary

apartheid   Official policy of racial segregation, involving political, legal, and economic discrimination against nonwhites, formerly practiced in the Republic of South Africa.

assassination   To murder a prominent person by surprise attack, usually for political reasons.

Black Muslim   A member of the Nation of Islam.

black nationalism   Militant black conviction of the need for separatism from whites and the establishment of self-governing black communities.

Black Panther Party   Organization of militant black Americans who advocated socialist reforms of government policies.

civil rights   Rights belonging to an individual by virtue of citizenship, including civil liberties, due process, equal protection under the law, and freedom from discrimination.

conk   To straighten hair using lye; once used by African Americans to make their hair look more "white."

Fruit of Islam   A group of Nation of Islam men trained in such forms of self-defense as karate and judo and used as a security team for the NOI.

hajj Pilgrimage to Mecca; an objective of the religious life of a Muslim.

hustler Person who does business in an illicit or unethical way.

infrastructure Underlying foundation or basic framework (as of a system or organization).

liberation Act or process of trying to achieve freedom from oppression.

Mecca City in western Saudi Arabia near the coast of the Red Sea; the birthplace of Mohammed, it is the holiest city of Islam and a pilgrimage site for all devout Muslims.

militant Combative and aggressive in the service of a cause.

mosque Islamic church or place of religious worship.

Muslim Believer in Islam.

nationalism Aspiration for national independence in a country under foreign domination; applied to African Americans under the domination of white America.

Nation of Islam (NOI) Religious organization founded by Elijah Muhammad for African Americans based on the teachings of Wallace Fard Muhammad (also called W. D. Fard) and some of the religious and cultural beliefs of traditional Islam.

nonviolence Policy of rejecting violence in favor of peaceful tactics as a means of gaining political objectives.

oppression Cruel exercise of power over people.

pan-Africanism   Belief that all of the nations of Africa should act together as one entity; extended by some thinkers to include African Americans in the United States.

racism   Discrimination or prejudice based on race.

revolutionary   Designed to bring about or support complete social change, or a person involved in the change process.

segregation   Separation of a race or class from the rest of society.

separatism   Belief in the separation of cultural, ethnic, or racial groups.

Southern Christian Leadership Conference (SCLC)   Led by Dr. Martin Luther King Jr., this group was instrumental in the struggle for civil rights and employed nonviolent forms of protest to achieve this goal.

Student Nonviolent Coordinating Committee (SNCC)   Mainly African American organization committed to nonviolent change of American discrimination against African Americans.

temple   Building dedicated to religious ceremonies or worship.

Universal Negro Improvement Association (UNIA)   Black separatist organization dedicated to African American liberation, founded in 1914 by Marcus Garvey.

For More Information

Organizations

Malcolm X Cultural Education Center
1227 Good Hope Road SE
Washington, DC 20020
e-mail: info@nationalmalcolmx.org
Web site: http://209.235.102.9/~nat12199/page2.html

Malcolm X Grassroots Movement
MXGM—Jackson
National Headquarters
P.O. Box 31762
Jackson, MS 39286
Web site: http://www.mxgrm.com

**National Association for the Advancement of
    Colored People (NAACP)**
4805 Mt. Hope Drive
Baltimore, MD 21215
(410) 521-4939
Web site: http://www.naacp.org

National Urban League
120 Wall Street
New York, NY 10005
(212) 558-5300
e-mail: info@nul.org
Web site: http://www.nul.org

Nation of Islam
7351 South Stoney Island Avenue
Chicago, IL 60649
(773) 324-6000
e-mail: email@noi.org
Web site: http://www.noi.org

Organization of African Unity
P.O. Box 3243
Addis Ababa, Ethiopia
+(251) 151-7700
Web site: http://www.oau-oua.org

Web Sites

Due to the changing nature of Internet links, the Rosen Publishing Group, Inc. has developed an online list of Web sites related to the subject of this book. This site is updated regularly. Please use this link to access the list:

http://www.rosenlinks.com/lpa/tamx

Films and Videos

Malcolm X. Directed by Spike Lee, 1992.

Malcolm X. Film documentary produced by Warner Brothers, 1972.

The Speeches of Collection: Speeches of Malcolm X. Produced by Mpi Home Video, 1997.

For Further Reading

Archer, Jules. *They Had a Dream: The Civil Rights Struggle from Frederick Douglass to Marcus Garvey to Martin Luther King and Malcolm X.* New York: Puffin Books, 1996.

Breitman, George, ed. *By Any Means Necessary.* New York: Pathfinder Press, 1970.

Breitman, George. *The Last Year of Malcolm X.* New York: Pathfinder Press, 1988.

Breitman, George, ed. *Malcolm X Speaks.* New York: Pathfinder Press, 1989.

Draper, Theodore. *The Rediscovery of Black Nationalism.* New York: Viking Press, 1970.

Evanzz, Karl. *The Judas Factor: The Plot to Kill Malcolm X.* New York: Thunder's Mouth Press, 1992.

Fanon, Frantz. *The Wretched of the Earth.* Translated by Constance Farrington. New York: Grove Press, 1968.

Farmer, James. *Lay Bare the Heart: An Autobiography of the Civil Rights Movement.* Fort Worth, TX: Texas Christian University Press, 1998.

Goldman, Peter. *The Death and Life of Malcolm X.* Urbana, IL: University of Illinois Press, 1979.

Karim, Benjamin, ed. *The End of White World Supremacy: Four Speeches by Malcolm X*. New York: Arcade Books, 1989.

King, Coretta Scott. *My Life with Martin Luther King, Jr.* Rev. ed. New York: Puffin Books, 1994.

Lincoln, C. Eric. *The Black Muslims in America.* 3rd ed. Grand Rapids, MI: W. B. Eerdsmans, 1993.

Lomax, Louis. *To Kill a Black Man*. Los Angeles: Holloway House Publishing Company, 1968.

Lomax, Louis. *The Negro Revolt*. New York: Signet Books, 1962.

Malcolm X, as told to Alex Haley. *The Autobiography of Malcolm X*. New York: Ballantine Books, 1992.

Perry, Bruce. *Malcolm: The Life of a Man Who Changed Black America*. Tarrytown, NY: Station Hill Press, 1991.

Perry, Bruce, ed. *Malcolm X: The Last Speeches*. New York: Pathfinder Press, 1989.

Warren, Robert Penn. *Who Speaks for the Negro?* New York: Vintage Books, 1965.

Index

A

Africa, 6, 8, 14, 22, 32, 34–35, 36, 37, 40
apartheid, 36–37

B

Black Muslims, 6, 8, 23, 26, 32, 44, 45
Black Panthers, 47
Butler, Norman 3X (aka Muhammad Abdul Aziz), 10, 39, 44–46, 48, 49–50

C

Central Intelligence Agency (CIA), 36, 37
civil rights movement, 5, 6, 8, 31
Congress of Racial Equality (CORE), 31

D

Davis, Ossie, 38, 41

F

Farrakhan, Louis, 48–50

G

Garvey, Marcus, 14
Goodman, Benjamin, 10–11

H

hajj, 32–33
Harlem, 9, 18, 25, 28, 31, 36, 38, 39, 49
Hayer, Talmadge (aka Thomas Hagan), 10, 12, 39, 42, 44, 45–46, 48

I

integration, 5, 7
Islam/Muslims, 6, 8, 19, 29, 32, 35

J

Johnson, Thomas 15X (aka Khalil Islam), 10, 44–46, 48

K

King, Dr. Martin Luther, Jr., 8, 47, 50

Index

L

Little, Reverend Earl, 14–16

M

Malcolm X
  aftermath of his assassina-
    tion, 38–40, 42, 50
  assassination of, 8, 9–13,
    36, 37, 47
  beliefs of, 22–23, 28,
    30–32, 50
  break from Nation of Islam,
    8, 32, 36, 44, 48
  children of, 9, 11, 36, 49
  comments about John F.
    Kennedy, 31, 39
  hajj to Mecca and travels to
    Africa and Middle East,
    8, 32–35, 36
  in jail, 18, 19–22, 29
  name change to El-Hajj Malik
    El-Shabazz, 8, 51
  name change to Malcolm X,
    7, 24
  and Nation of Islam, 8, 23,
    24–32
  police investigation of/trial
    for his assassination,
    39–40, 42–46, 48
  starting Muslim Mosque,
    Inc., 9, 32
  theories about his assassina-
    tion, 36–37, 40, 48–49
  youth as Malcolm Little, 7,
    14–23

Mecca, 8, 33, 34
Middle East, 6, 8, 32, 34
Muhammad, Elijah, 22, 23, 24,
    25, 26, 29–30, 31, 32,
    38–39, 44
Muhammad Speaks, 28, 36, 49

N

National Association for the
    Advancement of Colored
    People (NAACP), 31
Nation of Islam (NOI), 6–7, 8,
    10, 19, 22, 23, 24, 26, 28,
    29, 30, 34, 36, 38, 39, 40,
    44, 45, 46, 48, 50
  Fruit of Islam, 26, 38, 39

P

pan-African unity, 35, 51

R

Roberts, Gene, 12, 13

S

segregation, 5, 37
separatism, 5–6, 8, 50
Shabazz, Betty, 8, 9, 11, 13, 36, 49
Shabazz, Qubilah, 49
Southern Christian Leadership
    Conference (SCLC), 31
Student Nonviolent
    Coordinating Committee
    (SNCC), 47
Students for a Democratic
    Society (SDS), 47

About the Author

Allison Stark Draper has written books for young people on such history topics as the American Revolution, the California missions, and World War II. She lives in New York.

Photo Credits

Cover photo and p. 33 © John Launois/Black Star/TimePix; pp. 1, 4, 39, 49 © AP/Wide World Photos; p. 12 © AP/WCBS-TV; pp. 13, 17, 19, 30, 37, 41, 43, 45 (left), 45 (right) © Bettmann/Corbis; pp. 15, 23, 25, 28 © Hulton/Archive; p. 51 © Jacqes M. Chenet/Corbis.

Series Design and Layout

Les Kanturek